THE PLAYLET SERIES

FEAR

AF221220

An English play in 9 scenes about FEAR

For Years 9, 10 and 11 (Level 5/1)

By John Middleton

Bibliografische Information der Deutschen
Nationalbibliothek:
Die Deutsche Nationalbibliothek verzeichnet diese
Publikation in der Deutschen Nationalbibliografie;
detaillierte bibliografische Daten sind im Internet über
http://dnb.dnb.de abrufbar.

Herstellung und Verlag: BoD – Books on Demand,
Norderstedt

ISBN: 9783752627220

Other plays from THE PLAYLET SERIES by John Middleton:

EVERY DAY – a play in 10 scenes about EVERYDAY LIFE
for Years 2, 3 and 4 (Level 1/1)

FRIENDS – a play in 9 scenes about FRIENDS
for Years 3, 4 and 5 (Level 2/1)

NEW KEY CHAIN – a play in 15 scenes about KEYS
for Years 6, 7 and 8 (Level 3/1)

LUCKY CHARMS – a play in 10 scenes about LUCK
for Years 6, 7 and 8 (Level 3/2)

STAND UP – a play in 8 scenes about MORAL COURAGE
for Years 8, 9 and 10 (Level 4/1)

MONOLOGUES FOR YOUNG ADULTS – 25 scenes
for Years 11 and 12 or for university students (September 2020)

CONTENTS

FOREWORD

FEAR is a play for students in Years 9, 10 or 11 (Level 5/1). It is designed for a normal-sized English class and for students with varying interests in acting. Since there are 36 roles – none of which are really minor – students who enjoy acting can perform in several scenes and play to their heart's content, whereas students who aren't particularly keen on acting only have one role to master in one single scene. Every scene deals with a situation in which FEAR takes center stage. The themes are geared to the experiences of students today and offer young actresses and actors the opportunity to discover FEAR in its many guises while performing. The plots range from believable to supernatural, often straddling the gap between real objects of fear and the darker side of the human psyche. The language is idiomatic and accessible for advanced English learners. FEAR works well when performed for smaller audiences: parents and other classes. But it can also be highly entertaining for a large audience. Performing time: about 90 minutes. Of course, it is also possible to select individual scenes and perform them as simple skits outside the context of FEAR. In that case it is still recommendable to create a suitable setting for presenting the skits to an audience. The true joy of performing a foreign-language play is to feel it click, to realize that the people watching the performance don't only "get the picture", they are also delighted to see a story come to life when presented in English by non-native performers.

– John Middleton, Hamburg, 2020

SCENE 1   8 MINUTES AND 46 SECONDS

We may discover the only thing more detrimental than doing nothing is doing a tiny bit and thinking that's enough.

(If possible, the entire scene should last 8 minutes and 46 seconds. Flashing red and blue lights. A girl is standing in front of the audience, staring at one particular spot or person. She can't believe her eyes. She is witnessing something that deeply shocks her, possibly for the first time. She doesn't know what to do. Should she look away? Should she leave? Should she say something? Other people pass by behind her, they stop and look: a boy with a skateboard, a boy with headphones, a girl with shopping bags, a boy pushing a bike, a girl with a baby carriage. The girl standing in front takes out her cell phone, scrolls and touches something on her display. Then she holds the phone up and starts filming. She squints now and then.)

BOY WITH A SKATEBOARD *(looks around)*

What's going on?

GIRL WITH A PHONE *(looking at an imaginary victim "on the street" – in the audience)*

There's a guy lying on the street.

GIRL WITH SHOPPING BAGS *(looking at the imaginary victim)* What's wrong with him? Is he injured?

GIRL WITH A BABY CARRIAGE *(looking at the imaginary victim)* Maybe.

GIRL WITH SHOPPING BAGS *(looking at the imaginary victim)* He's handcuffed.

BOY WITH HEADPHONES *(slides his headphones down around his neck, looking at the imaginary victim)*

There's a cop kneeling on his neck.

BOY WITH A BIKE *(looking at the imaginary victim)*

What did he do?

BOY WITH HEADPHONES *(looking at the imaginary victim)*

The cop?

11

BOY WITH A BIKE *(looking at the imaginary victim)*
The guy on the street.
BOY WITH HEADPHONES *(looking at the imaginary victim)*
The guy with the cop on his neck?
BOY WITH A BIKE
Yeah. What did he do?
GIRL WITH A BABY CARRIAGE
No idea. Must have done something.
GIRL WITH SHOPPING BAGS
Like what?
GIRL WITH A BABY CARRIAGE
Don't know. People are always doing stuff.
BOY WITH HEADPHONES
But why's the cop kneeling on his neck?
GIRL WITH A BABY CARRIAGE
Probably resisted.
BOY WITH HEADPHONES
How can you resist with your hands cuffed?
GIRL WITH A BABY CARRIAGE
Maybe he said stuff.
GIRL WITH SHOPPING BAGS
Like what?
GIRL WITH A BABY CARRIAGE
Maybe he badmouthed the cop.
BOY WITH A SKATEBOARD
Maybe he gave the cop a threatening, dehumanizing look.
GIRL WITH A BABY CARRIAGE
What are you talking about?
BOY WITH A SKATEBOARD
Maybe he sneered at the cop.
BOY WITH A BIKE
They can't arrest you for sneering.

BOY WITH A SKATEBOARD

Maybe he smelled bad. Maybe he walked too slow. Maybe his tail lights weren't working. Maybe he was black…

GIRL WITH A BABY CARRIAGE

Maybe, maybe, maybe. Maybe he did something wrong.

GIRL WITH SHOPPING BAGS

Like what?

GIRL WITH A BABY CARRIAGE

I don't know. Lots of stuff.

BOY WITH A SKATEBOARD

Loitering, jaywalking, illegal possession of drugs, disorderly conduct, paying with a forged 20-dollar bill, refusing to be lynched…

BOY WITH HEADPHONES

Stop-and-frisk.

GIRL WITH SHOPPING BAGS

What?

BOY WITH HEADPHONES

The cops can stop you on the street and search you for no real reason…

GIRL WITH SHOPPING BAGS

For no real reason?

BOY WITH A SKATEBOARD

If you're white, that's all right.

BOY WITH HEADPHONES

If you're black, stay back.

GIRL HOLDING A PHONE

Racial profiling.

GIRL WITH SHOPPING BAGS

What?

BOY WITH HEADPHONES

It's when the cops target you, 'cause you're black.

BOY WITH A SKATEBOARD

Most black people who get stopped by the cops weren't even doing anything wrong.

BOY WITH HEADPHONES

Nine out of ten.

GIRL WITH SHOPPING BAGS

What?

BOY WITH HEADPHONES

Nine out of ten blacks who get stopped by the cops are innocent.

GIRL WITH A BABY CARRIAGE

What if they're carrying a gun? I've heard that…

GIRL HOLDING A PHONE

He's saying something.

GIRL WITH SHOPPING BAGS

What's he saying?

(Silence. Everyone listens.)

GIRL WITH A PHONE

No idea.

GIRL WITH SHOPPING BAGS

Is he breathing?

GIRL WITH A BABY CARRIAGE

What do you mean?

BOY WITH HEADPHONES

Is he breathing with the cop on his neck?

GIRL WITH A BABY CARRIAGE

If you can talk you can breathe.

BOY WITH A SKATEBOARD

What?

GIRL WITH A BABY CARRIAGE

That's what the policeman said.

BOY WITH A SKATEBOARD

What?

GIRL WITH A BABY CARRIAGE

"You're fine. You're talking fine," he said.

GIRL WITH A PHONE

He said he can't breathe.

GIRL WITH SHOPPING BAGS

The policeman?

BOY WITH HEADPHONES

The guy on the street.

GIRL WITH A BABY CARRIAGE

What's the policeman doing now?

BOY WITH A BIKE

Which one?

GIRL WITH A BABY CARRIAGE

What do you mean?

BOY WITH A BIKE

There are four cops.

GIRL WITH A BABY CARRIAGE

Four?

BOY WITH HEADPHONES

One on his neck and three standing around.

GIRL WITH A BABY CARRIAGE

What's the one on his neck doing now?

GIRL WITH A PHONE

He has his hands in his pockets.

BOY WITH A SKATEBOARD

And he's digging his knee into the guy's throat.

BOY WITH HEADPHONES

He's smiling.

GIRL WITH A PHONE *(speaking to the imaginary policeman)*

Hey!

(Silence)

Didn't you hear the guy? He said he can't breathe.

BOY WITH A SKATEBOARD *(to the imaginary policeman)*

You think that's okay? Check his pulse.

BOY WITH HEADPHONES

He ain't moved yet, bro. He ain't moved. Not once. Is he gonna kill him?

GIRLWITH A PHONE *(to the imaginary policeman)*

Hey, he isn't moving.

GIRL WITH SHOPPING BAGS

Did they just kill him?

GIRL WITH A PHONE

No, he said he's scared or something like that.

GIRL WITH A BABY CARRIAGE

Who?

GIRL WITH A PHONE

The guy on the street.

BOY WITH A SKATEBOARD *(to the imaginary policeman)*

Let him get up! He's not a bad guy.

GIRL WITH A BABY CARRIAGE

How do you know? Maybe he has a gun.

BOY WITH HEADPHONES

They already frisked him.

GIRL WITH A BABY CARRIAGE

Maybe he'll take the policeman's gun and start shooting. I heard about this black guy once that took a policeman's weapon and...

BOY WITH HEADPHONES

How can he take the cop's gun with his hands cuffed behind his back?

BOY WITH A BIKE

He's trying to talk. What's he saying?

GIRL WITH A PHONE

He's scared. He's claustrophobic. He can't breathe.

GIRL WITH A BABY CARRIAGE *(to the imaginary man lying on the street)*

Stop talking! It takes a heck of a lot of oxygen to talk. Stop yelling!

BOY WITH HEADPHONES

He ain't yelling. He's dying.

BOY WITH A BIKE *(to the imaginary man lying on the street)*

You can't win, man. You can't win.

GIRL WITH A BABY CARRIAGE

What are you talking about?

GIRL WITH A PHONE *(to the imaginary policeman)*

He isn't resisting, Officer. He says he's sorry.

BOY WITH A BIKE

What did he just say?

GIRL WITH A PHONE

He's begging the cop not to shoot him. He says he just lost his mom.

BOY WITH A BIKE *(to the imaginary policemen)*

Excuse me, excuse me, Officer… Can't one of you roll the man onto his side, so he can breathe?

GIRL WITH A PHONE

He says there's no need to.

BOY WITH A BIKE

Who?

GIRL WITH A PHONE

The cop.

GIRL WITH SHOPPING BAGS

No need to do what?

BOY WITH A SKATEBOARD

Didn't he say something about his mom?

GIRL WITH SHOPPING BAGS

He said he just lost her.

GIRL WITH A PHONE

He said, "Mama, I love you. I can't do nothing…"

BOY WITH A BIKE *(to the imaginary man lying on the street)*

Hey man, just get up and get in the car.

GIRL WITH A PHONE

He can't move.

BOY WITH A BIKE *(to the imaginary policeman)*

Hey, Officer, his nose is bleeding.

BOY WITH HEADPHONES *(to the imaginary policeman)*

Get off his neck, bro. He's a human.

BOY WITH A SKATEBOARD *(to the imaginary policeman)*

You got him down, man. Let him breathe at least.

GIRL WITH SHOPPING BAGS *(to the imaginary policeman)*

This is wrong. You got your feet right on his neck.

BOY WITH A BIKE

You having fun, Officer? *(to the imaginary policeman)*

BOY WITH HEADPHONES *(to the imaginary policeman)*

You're a tough guy, bro. He ain't even resisting arrest.

GIRL WITH SHOPPING BAGS *(to the imaginary policeman)*

How long do you have to hold him down?

GIRL WITH A BABY CARRIAGE

That's why you shouldn't do drugs.

GIRL WITH A PHONE

This is not about drugs.

BOY WITH HEADPHONES *(to the imaginary policeman)*

You think you're cool, man? You're stopping his damn breathing.

BOY WITH A BIKE *(moves closer to the audience)*

What's your badge number, Officer?

BOY WITH HEADPHONES *(to boy with a bike)*

Careful, bro. Don't get too close. Those cops are trigger-happy.

GIRL WITH SHOPPING BAGS

What's wrong with those guys?

BOY WITH A SKATEBOARD

What guys?

GIRL WITH SHOPPING BAGS

The cops.

BOY WITH HEADPHONES *(to the imaginary policeman)*

I'm not scared of you wimps!

(The boy with the headphones looks around and ducks behind the others.)

GIRL WITH SHOPPING BAGS

What's the cop taking out of his pocket?

BOY WITH A SKATEBOARD

Mace…

BOY WITH HEADPHONES *(hiding behind the others)*

Pepper spray! Watch out!

GIRL WITH A PHONE *(to the imaginary policeman)*

Check his pulse… right now!

GIRL WITH SHOPPING BAGS

What's wrong with them?

GIRL WITH A BABY CARRIAGE

Just let 'em do their job!

BOY WITH A SKATEBOARD *(to girl with a baby carriage)*

What's your problem?

(The girl with a baby carriage looks at her "baby" and moves behind the others.)

GIRL WITH A PHONE *(to girl with a baby carriage)*

If you are not part of the solution, you're part of the problem.

GIRL WITH A BABY CARRIAGE

What problem?

GIRL WITH A PHONE

Look at this!

(She points at her phone's display.)

GIRL WITH SHOPPING BAGS *(moving closer to look)*
What?
(All the others – except for the girl with the baby carriage – move in closer to look at the display.)
GIRL WITH A PHONE
Look!
(She holds up her phone, so they can see the display.)
GIRL WITH A BABY CARRIAGE
What about it?
GIRL WITH A PHONE *(looking at the display)*
That's the problem.
GIRL WITH A BABY CARRIAGE
I don't get it.
BOY WITH A SKATEBOARD *(looking at the display)*
Get off the man's neck!
BOY WITH A BIKE *(looking at the display)*
Does he have a pulse? Check his pulse, damn it!
GIRL WITH A PHONE *(looking at the display)*
No response.
BOY WITH HEADPHONES *(looking at the display)*
Pulse! Bro, he isn't moving!
GIRL WITH SHOPPING BAGS *(looking at the display)*
Are you going to keep sitting on his neck like that?
GIRL WITH A BABY CARRIAGE *(looking at something in the audience)*
Hey!
BOY WITH HEADPHONES *(looking at the display)*
Pulse! Pulse! Pulse!
GIRL WITH A BABY CARRIAGE *(looking around at the others on stage)*
Hey guys!
GIRL WITH SHOPPING BAGS *(to the imaginary policeman)*
Are you trying to kill him?

GIRL WITH A BABY CARRIAGE *(looking around at the others on stage)*

Didn't you guys see that policeman over there waving his hands? We'd better do what he says.

GIRL WITH SHOPPING BAGS

What cop? Where?

GIRL WITH A BABY CARRIAGE

The policeman, the Asian guy, the one with the gun. We'd better do what he says.

(Everybody looks at one particular point in the audience, then they slowly start backing up - except for the girl with a phone. Silence.)

GIRL WITH A PHONE *(stands alone in front, still looking at the display on her phone)*

What's going on here? Who are we? What are we doing?
Silence)

GIRL WITH A PHONE *(still looking at the display)*

What are we doing? What's this all about?

GIRL WITH A BABY CARRIAGE

It's just a normal, everyday arrest. That's why the police are here.

GIRL WITH SHOPPING BAGS

They're killing that guy.

GIRL WITH A BABY CARRIAGE

They're arresting him, 'cause he did something wrong.

BOY WITH A BIKE

And the cops?

GIRL WITH A BABY CARRIAGE

What about the cops?

GIRL WITH A PHONE *(still looking at the display)*

What if the cops are doing something wrong?

GIRL WITH A BABY CARRIAGE

What do you mean?

GIRL WITH A PHONE *(still looking at the display)*
What do we do? Who do we call?
GIRL WITH A BABY CARRIAGE
What?
GIRL WITH A PHONE *(still looking at the display)*
If the cops do something wrong…
BOY WITH A BIKE
Yeah. How do we police the police?
BOY WITH A SKATEBOARD
How do we deal with institutional injustice?
GIRL WITH SHOPPING BAGS
Racial harassment?
BOY WITH A SKATEBOARD
400 years of grief, 400 years of killing black bodies.
BOY WITH A BIKE
It's structural. It's a pattern.
GIRL WITH A PHONE *(still looking at the display)*
Something underneath white skin goes pop when it sees black.
BOY WITH A SKATEBOARD
The cheapness of a black life.
GIRL WITH A BABY CARRIAGE
Accept it.
GIRL WITH SHOPPING BAGS
Accept what?
GIRL WITH A BABY CARRIAGE
Some lives matter more than others. That's the way it is.
BOY WITH HEADPHONES
And some statues matter more than lives.
GIRL WITH A BABY CARRIAGE
What are you talking about?

BOY WITH HEADPHONES
Groups of armed white men defending statues of slave owners.

GIRL WITH A BABY CARRIAGE
Brave men defending our culture from terrorist assaults.

BOY WITH HEADPHONES *(moves to the side of the group and stands alone, raises his fist)*
Bullshit, bullshit, bullshit! Tear down the symbols of white supremacy!

GIRL WITH A BABY CARRIAGE *(to boy with headphones)*
And destroy our own lives?

BOY WITH HEADPHONES *(to girl with a baby carriage)*
What are you talking about?

GIRL WITH A BABY CARRIAGE *(to boy with headphones)*
White privilege! You should thank God you were born white, so you can do whatever you want.

BOY WITH HEADPHONES *(to girl with a baby carriage)*
What are you talking about?

GIRL WITH A PHONE *(still looking at the display)*
She's right.

GIRL WITH A BABY CARRIAGE *(to boy with headphones)*
You love your privileges, don't you, white boy?

BOY WITH HEADPHONES *(to girl with a baby carriage)*
Bullshit! What privileges?

BOY WITH A BIKE *(to boy with headphones)*
You live where you want.

CHORUS *(everyone but boy with headphones)*
Without harassment.

GIRL WITH SHOPPING BAGS *(to boy with headphones)*
Go to school where you want.

CHORUS
Without harassment.

BOY WITH A SKATEBOARD *(to girl with a baby carriage)*

Get the job you want.

CHORUS

Without harassment.

GIRL WITH A PHONE *(still looking at the display)*

Jog where you want.

CHORUS

Without harassment.

BOY WITH A BIKE *(to girl with a baby carriage)*

Drive your car where you want.

CHORUS

Without harassment.

GIRL WITH SHOPPING BAGS *(to girl with a baby carriage)*

Shop where you want.

CHORUS

Without harassment.

GIRL WITH A PHONE *(still looking at the display)*

You are surrounded by media that mirrors your whiteness.

BOY WITH A BIKE *(to girl with a baby carriage)*

The cops believe you, because you are white.

GIRL WITH A BABY CARRIAGE *(to girl with a baby carriage)*

Your kids don't get harassed, because they're white.

BOY WITH HEADPHONES

I don't have any kids!

GIRL WITH SHOPPING BAGS *(to girl with a baby carriage)*

And the founding fathers are your founding fathers.

GIRL WITH A BABY CARRIAGE

Because they were white, too. Wake up, jerk. It is what it is, a white world. And you're white.

BOY WITH A BIKE *(like an announcer at a tennis match)*

Advantage white boy!

BOY WITH HEADPHONES

Disadvantage black boy!

GIRL WITH A PHONE *(turning her head to look at boy with headphones)*

And his disadvantage is your advantage.

GIRL WITH SHOPPING BAGS *(looking at the imaginary victim in the audience)*

What's happening?

(She points her finger at the spot where the victim was lying. Everybody turns to see. We hear an ambulance siren, loud at first, then subsiding. Everyone except the girl with a phone "watches it leave" – from left to right. Then they leave the stage in different directions.

GIRL WITH A PHONE *(stops filming and checks the time on her phone)*

8 minutes and 46 seconds.

(She pockets her phone and quickly leaves the stage.)

SCENE 2   MESSAGE IN A GADGET (Part 1)

Any similarities between the statements made in this playlet and clues published by a global conspiracy theory are purely coincidental.

(A desk with a sign "MESSAGE IN A GADGET – REGISTER

HERE". A young woman in business attire is sitting behind a desk.

A young man wearing a protective mask approaches the desk, he is

holding a mounted fish.)

RECEPTIONIST 1 *(without looking up)*

Can I help you?

YOUNG MAN *(rather shy)*

Yes, uh, I'm not sure, uh, you see...

RECEPTIONIST 1 *(still busy looking at something on her desk)*

Yes?

YOUNG MAN *(looking at the sign)*

This is, uh, the place where you register gadgets with, uh...

RECEPTIONIST 1 *(looking up and pointing to the sign)*

What does it say?

YOUNG MAN *(reading the sign)*

Uh... "Message in a, uh, gadget – uh, register here"

RECEPTIONIST 1 *(moves her hand across her face)*

What's that thing on your face?

YOUNG MAN

What?

RECEPTIOINST 1 *(circling her mouth with her hand)*

That thing covering your face. I can't see you.

YOUNG MAN

Oh, my mask?

RECEPTIONIST 2

Thank you.

YOUNG MAN

Don't you believe in wearing masks?

RECEPTIONIST 1

Do you see one?

YOUNG MAN *(shaking his head)*

Why not?

RECEPTIONIST 1

They do absolutely nothing to protect you.

YOUNG MAN

Are you a scientist?

RECEPTIONIST 1

No, I've done tons of reading.

YOUNG MAN

Are you a doctor?

RECEPTIONIST 1 *(looking at something on her desk again)*

Can I help you?

YOUNG MAN *(holding up his mounted fish)*

You see, I bought this fish…

RECEPTIONIST 1 *(looking at something on her desk and writing)*

Yes?

YOUNG MAN

It's supposed to, uh, sing and dance on the wall, when you
hang it up, uh, like this *(holds it up against an imaginary wall)*.

RECEPTIONIST 1 *(continues writing something on the desk)*

Yes?

YOUNG MAN *(points to a button under the fish)*

But when I push the button instead of singing, it starts to…

RECEPTIONIST 1 *(looking up for a short moment)*

Complaints next door, please. Now if you don't mind…

*(The receptionist looks down again, shaking her head. The young
man pushes the button under the fish. The fish starts to wiggle and
"speak – the "voicemail" should be loud, the voice should have a
mysterious quality, the recording should have some static in the
background.)*

FISH *(wiggling and still being held up by the young man)*

The destruction of the global cabal is imminent.

RECEPTIONIST 1 *(looking up)*

Excuse me, what did you just say?

YOUNG MAN

Not me. The, uh, the fish. Voicemail, the message in the
gadget.

RECEPTIONIST 1 *(looking at the fish)*

The fish?

(The young man presses the button again.)

FISH *(wiggling)*

Breadcrumbs... every dog has its day... deep state...

YOUNG MAN *(confused, still holding the mounted fish)*

I don't understand...

RECEPTIONIST 1 *(jumping up, taking the fish and placing it on her desk, intense)*

Be quiet! Don't you realize how important this is! Where we go one, we go all.

(She starts writing something down, then pushes the button under the fish.)

FISH *(wiggling)*

Death squads... Biden... Hillary Clinton... the storm... follow the white rabbit, child-eating pedophiles.

YOUNG MAN *(even more confused)*

The fish keeps talking about the, uh, white rabbit...

RECEPTIONIST *(annoyed, becoming frantic)*

Shut up! This is red alert!

(She pushes the button under the fish again.)

FISH *(wiggling)*

Banks control people. Governments control people. Ready to play?

YOUNG MAN

Play what?

RECEPTIONIST *(shocked)*

Oh my God! We are at war!

(The receptionist pushes the button under the fish again.)

FISH *(wiggling)*

We are fighting for life. We are fighting for good. Nothing is a coincidence.

RECEPTIONIST

Fear is real. Dark to light. Together you are stronger, digital soldiers!

YOUNG MAN *(more confused than ever)*

Is this fake news?

RECEPTIONIST *(pushing the button under the fish again)*

You are learning.

FISH *(wiggling)*

Undeniable, unpredictable, unrestricted. Seals broken. Future proves past. Only the tip! Only the tip! Access granted!

RECEPTIONIST *(picking up the phone, and speaking frantically)*

Betrayed! We are in the final stage. Clowns in China! Breadcrumbs! Breadcrumbs! Nothing is as it seems! We see all! We hear all! The storm! The great awakening! Arrests! Mass executions! We are the puppet masters!

YOUNG MAN

Fake news?

RECEPTIONIST *(raising her fist and screaming)*

Danger! SOS! No one is safe anymore! Evacuate, evacuate! They say they have a bomb!

(The receptionist runs off stage, and the young man watches her go, then he picks up the fish and pushes the button. The fish starts wiggling and singing a song.)

YOUNG MAN *(delighted)*

Oh wow, it works. How cool.

(The young man looks in the direction where the receptionist disappeared.)

YOUNG MAN *(shouting after the receptionist)*

Hey, thanks for your help! Everything's fine now!

(We suddenly hear an air-raid siren. The young man looks up. We see search lights flashing across the ceiling and throughout the auditorium. Then we hear planes flying overhead and bombs falling. The young man takes his fish and runs off stage.)

SCENE 3   TO PHOBIA OR NOT TO PHOBIA

The excerpts read in this playlet are from the Internet essay "Fears and Phobias" at the KidsHealth website from Nemours Children's Health System. (https://kidshealth.org/en/teens/phobias.html#catfriends).

(A park bench. Josh, an adolescent, casually dressed, is reading a book.)

JOSH *(reading aloud)*

"Fear is one of the most basic human emotions… From the time we are infants, we are equipped with the survival instincts necessary to respond with fear when we sense danger or feel unsafe."

(We hear screeching tires, the dramatic sounds of a car crash, blood-curdling screams. Josh looks up for a moment, only mildly curious, then he smiles, returns to the book and continues reading.)

"But sometimes a fear is unnecessary and causes more caution than the situation calls for."

(A boy with a rolled-up sleeve frantically runs across the stage, followed by a person in a doctor's white coat with a large syringe. Once again Josh looks up, only mildly curious. He watches the chase.)

BOY WITH A ROLLED-UP SLEEVE *(running forwards, looking anxiously over his shoulder)*

No! No! Help! Please don't! Leave me alone! Don't touch me! Help! Help!

DOCTOR IN A WHITE COAT *(running after the boy, holding up a large syringe)*

Wait! Stop! It's just a little prick! It won't hurt!

BOY WITH A ROLLED-UP SLEEVE

Help! Go away! Leave me alone!

DOCTOR IN A WHITE COAT

It's for your own good! You don't want to get Corona, do you?

(The boy with a rolled-up sleeve and the doctor in a white coat run off stage. Josh smiles again, returns to the book and continues reading.)

JOSH *(reading aloud)*

"Someone might develop a bee phobia after being stung... For that person, looking at a photograph of a bee, seeing a bee from a distance, or even walking near flowers where there *could* be a bee can all trigger the phobia."

(We hear a dog barking. A girl suddenly appears and jumps on the bench. She stands beside Josh who is still sitting. It is Susannah. She is wearing protective clothing on her legs, torso and arms, and she has an unusual looking helmet on her head with a face mask – might be an American football helmet. She seems frightened as she stands on her tiptoes. Josh looks up, only mildly curious. Susannah looks down at him.)

SUSANNAH

I hope you don't mind, but I thought I heard barking.

JOSH

Oh, I didn't notice.

(Silence.)

JOSH

Afraid of dogs?

SUSANNAH *(shrieking)*

Ahhh! Petrified.

JOSH

A personal experience?

SUSANNAH

Cynophobia.

JOSH

How long?

SUSANNAH

My whole life.

JOSH

Genetics?

SUSANNAH

No, my brother showed me a gruesome video when I was little.

JOSH

Dog attack?

SUSANNAH *(shrieks)*

Ahh! *(then nods, nervously moving her weight from one foot to the other)* Lots of blood.

JOSH

Pit bulls?

SUSANNAH *(shrieks)*

Ahh! *(then squeezes her hands, rubs her cheeks)* Yeah.

JOSH

Kids and…

SUSANNAH *(shrieks)*

Ahh! *(then interrupts him, pleading)* Oh God, don't remind me!

JOSH *(trying to calm her)*

Just breathe deeply.

SUSANNAH *(getting jumpy, almost having a panic attack)*

Yes… in through the nose, purse the lips, out through the mouth, in through the nose, purse the lips, out through the mouth…

(Susannah breathes deeply, in and out, in and out, several times.)

JOSH

And since then?

SUSANNAH *(sitting down on the bench)*

The moment I hear barking…

JOSH

Or someone simply mentions a dog?

SUSANNAH *(shrieking)*

Ahh! *(nodding)* Yeah. You know, I literally get sick when I see one on television.

JOSH

Ever tried exposure therapy?

SUSANNAH

That's just it. I never got past looking at a picture.

JOSH

No actual exposure to a real... you-know-what?

SUSANNAH

I just have to say the word, and I panic.

JOSH

Relaxation training?

SUSANNAH

Mindfulness meditation?

JOSH

Yeah.

SUSANNAH

Like listening to the trees rustling in the wind?

JOSH

Yeah.

SUSANNAH

Observing colors?

JOSH

Yeah. Does it calm you?

SUSANNAH

Sure, as long as I don't think of a you-know-what.

JOSH

Medication?

SUSANNAH

Prozac, Luvox, Zoloft...

JOSH

Celxa, Lexapro?

SUSANNAH

Tried them all.

JOSH

Half-smiling?

SUSANNAH

Excuse me?

JOSH

Half-smiling – raising the corners of your mouth and…

SUSANNAH

Oh yeah, I tried that, too…

JOSH *(acting and talking like a therapist)*

"Allow yourself to feel calm and tranquil as your mind is quiet and peaceful."

(Susannah closes her eyes and immediately goes into meditation mode.)

SUSANNAH

"Imagine yourself in a place which makes you feel serene."

JOSH

"A quiet moonlit beach, with waves gently lapping on the shore."

SUSANNAH

"A beautiful garden scene on a spring day with colorful flowers everywhere."

JOSH

"Let serenity permeate your whole experience."

SUSANNAH *(struggling to achieve serenity)*

"And gently raise the corners of your mouth…"

JOSH

"Now imagine yourself in a threatening circumstance, a situation that would normally cause fear and panic. Imagine that you replace those feelings with a serene half-smile…"

SUSANNAH *(shakes her head, then opens her eyes)*

The problem is that they never smile back.

JOSH

What?

SUSANNAH

They never smile back.

JOSH

The you-know-whats?

SUSANNAH *(nodding)*

No matter how much I half-smile, they never smile back.

JOSH

Actually, you-know-whats can be trained to smile, but a smiley you-know-what doesn't necessarily mean it's happy...

(Once again we hear a dog bark. Susannah jumps up. She holds her throat in panic.)

SUSANNAH *(shrieking)*

Ahh! Ahh! Ahh!

JOSH

Just relax...

(We hear more barking, it seems to be getting closer.)

SUSANNAH *(shrieking)*

Ahh! Ahh!

(Susannah runs off stage. Josh watches her go, then half-smiles and returns to his book.)

JOSH *(reading aloud)*

"Certain fears are normal during childhood..."

(Suddenly something moves under the bench. Josh looks up, strangely aware of something going on underneath him. We are also surprised, because we hadn't really noticed that someone or something was hidden beneath a blanket under the bench and is now cautiously emerging from their hiding-place.)

JOSH *(continuing)*

"Young kids often have fears of the dark, being alone, strangers and monsters or other scary, imaginary creatures."

(A boy, Ron, shyly removes the blanket, straightens up, meticulously folds the blanket and places it on the bench next to Josh.)

JOSH *(glancing at Ron, as he continues to read)*

"School-aged kids might be afraid when it's stormy…"

(Lights flash on and off to symbolize lightning, several loud claps of thunder. Ron frantically gets on the bench next to Josh and cowers with his arms around his knees.)

"As they grow and learn… most kids are able to slowly conquer these fears and outgrow them."

(Ron has buried his head between his knees, as he continues to sit on the bench with his arms wrapped around his ankles. Josh gets up and moves behind the bench.)

JOSH *(looking at Ron)*

Want to talk?

(Silence, Ron doesn't move.)

JOSH

I have time.

(Silence. Ron releases his hands around his ankles and puts his feet on the ground/floor.)

JOSH

Autophobia?

(Ron looks up, he gazes at Josh for a moment, then nods.)

JOSH

My younger sister suffers from it.

RON

Really bad?

JOSH

It used to be really bad, but she's doing much better now. She's more or less developed her own therapy.

RON

She probably still has some bad days though, doesn't she?

JOSH

You're right.

(Josh sits down on the bench again.)

JOSH

Just a couple of nights ago she had this recurring dream – part of her therapy is to keep a dream journal, and she sometimes shows me what she wrote.

RON

About being abandoned?

JOSH

What?

RON

Was it a dream about being abandoned?

JOSH

Yes, it was. She dreamt that we had driven to some old deserted railway tower out in the middle of nowhere.

RON

With your family?

JOSH

Yeah, my younger sister, my parents and me.

RON

You have an older sister, too?

JOSH

Yeah, but she wasn't with us.

RON

Did she go up?

JOSH

Who?

RON

Did your younger sister go up to the top of the tower?

JOSH

Yeah, we all did. There were these rickety old stairs, and there was no glass in the windows.

RON

And suddenly she was all alone?

JOSH *(slightly surprised)*

Yeah, right. How do you know?

RON

At least once a week I basically have the same dream.

JOSH

You're kidding?

RON

In my case it's a deserted viewing platform in the mountains.

JOSH *(nodding)*

That's amazing.

RON

Then she probably looked out of a window and saw you and your parents drive away.

JOSH *(nodding)*

She said I waved to her before I got in the car.

(Both boys nod. Silence.)

RON

I was on my way home.

JOSH

From school?

RON *(nodding)*

My mom doesn't get home until midnight.

JOSH

Late shift?

RON *(nodding)*

You could call it that.

JOSH

Brothers? Sisters?

RON *(shaking his head)*

My dad left when I was four.

JOSH

Any contact?

RON

A birthday card…

JOSH

Every year?

RON

Sometimes.

Josh nods.)

JOSH

Must be tough.

RON *(nodding)*

You know, this is a good place to be.

JOSH

Here? On the bench?

RON

Under the bench. And on the bench.

JOSH

Lots of people? Lots of noise?

RON

Yeah.

JOSH

So this isn't the first time?

RON

I come here almost every day.

JOSH

Here?

RON

Uh-huh.

JOSH

To the bench?

RON

Or underneath. It all depends.

JOSH

On what?

RON

I know some of the regulars, and they know me.

JOSH

So you sit on the bench? With the regulars?

RON

Sometimes.

JOSH

And it helps?

RON

It distracts me.

JOSH

From yourself?

RON *(nodding)*

From thoughts.

JOSH

Like what?

RON

That my mom might go away and never come back. Or that I'm the only person in the world who's really alive, and everybody else is just playing along to make me think they're real.

JOSH

The Truman syndrome?

RON

Sort of. I have the feeling that someone is always filming me and uploading the films to youtube, which is why I spend half the night looking for film clips of myself on the Internet.

JOSH

You feel like people recognize you on the street?

RON

All the time.

JOSH

As if they knew something about you that you don't know?

RON *(nodding)*

When I was in 2nd grade I was always daydreaming, so one day the teacher decided to play a trick on me. She gave the class some instructions, she told us to get up and leave the classroom and go to the film room. But since I was off in my own little world, I didn't hear what she said, and I didn't notice that everyone else had left the room.

JOSH

You were all alone in the classroom?

RON *(nodding)*

When I realized that all the others had left, I started to cry. And that's when the teacher and the other students came back into the classroom and started laughing.

(While the two are talking, we see a girl several meters behind the bench. It is Lisa. She tiptoes towards Josh without him noticing. She has a medium-sized backpack on her back.)

JOSH

That was really mean.

RON

The teacher wanted to teach me a lesson.

JOSH

Looks like she taught you more than that.

RON

Yep.

(Lisa is now directly behind Josh. She pulls something out of her pocket. Ron catches a glimpse of her and turns his head to see.)

JOSH

Do you often have panic attacks?

RON

Only during a thunderstorm…

(Lisa drops something large and black and wobbly on Josh's lap. Josh jumps up and stands on the bench.)

JOSH *(brushing the large, black, wobbly thing from his lap and screaming)*

Ahh! A spider! Help!

(He jumps down and runs off stage.)

RON *(to Josh)*

What's wrong?

(Ron picks up the spider and looks at it.)

RON

A rubber spider? *(looks at Lisa)* I have one just like it.

LISA *(walks to the front of the bench and sits down)*

Josh hates spiders. Arachnophobia. He once jumped from his 2nd-floor bedroom window to get away from one.

RON

You're kidding?

LISA

Broke his foot.

RON *(handing Lisa the rubber spider)*

A real spider?

LISA *(shaking her head)*

A rubber one. But very realistic. Cost me a fortune.

RON

You have lots of spiders?

LISA

Real spiders and toy spiders.

RON *(pointing)*

And that boy?

LISA *(glancing to the side)*

Josh?

RON

Yeah?

LISA

My older brother.

RON

You sure don't look like brother and sister.

LISA

That's what everybody says.

RON

He told me about you.

LISA

Oh yeah? What did he say?

RON

That you have a phobia.

LISA

Sure, everybody has a phobia, don't they?

RON

What?

(Ron stares at Lisa.)

LISA *(Lisa looks Ron in the eyes)*

You have a phobia, too.

RON

How do you know?

LISA

Your eyes. I can see it.

RON

Really?

LISA

Autophobia, right?

RON *(hesitating, then nodding)*

Same as you.

(Lisa nods. Silence. Suddenly several claps of thunder. Ron starts to shake, he pulls his legs up and wraps his arms around his ankles in a cowering position.)

LISA *(not even looking at Ron)*

I used to react to thunder, too. It took me days to get back to normal again.

(Ron continues to cower.)

LISA

But that was before I discovered my one true love… spiders.

(Lisa takes off her backpack and opens it. Ron cautiously peers inside. Lisa takes out various covered glass jars, holding them up, so Ron can see them. Ron stops cowering and puts his feet back down on the ground/floor.)

LISA

Here.

(She hands some of the jars to Ron who seems fascinated, he holds up the jars and examines their contents from different angles.)

RON

They are really cool.

LISA

Black widows, brown recluse spiders, jumping spiders, wolf spiders…

RON

And tarantulas?

LISA

Sure thing.

RON

Really?

LISA *(taking a little box from her backpack*

Here.

(She gives the box to Ron. He carefully opens it and smiles.)

RON

Can I pet it?

LISA

Sure. If you like, you can take it home with you.

RON

And bring it back tomorrow?

LISA

Sure.

RON

What does it eat?

LISA

Insects. Lots of insects. Or baby mice if you have any.

RON *(smiling at her)*

What a shame. No baby mice today.

(Lisa and Ron both chuckle.)

LISA

See you tomorrow?

RON *(playing with the tarantula in the box)*

Same time, same place?

LISA *(nodding)*

The bench at 4 p.m. I'll bring my Brazilian wandering spider.

RON

Sounds cool. Never seen one before. Isn't that one of the world's deadliest spiders?

LISA

The deadliest.

(Lisa and Ron exchange looks and nod.)

And always remember. To phobia or not to phobia, that is the question.

(Lisa gets up and leaves. As if on cue, several claps of thunder again. Ron looks up but only smiles. Then he pets the tarantula.)

RON *(in a soothing voice)*

Don't worry, little fella. Everything's all right. It's just a bit of thunder.

SCENE 4   MESSAGE IN A GADGET (Part 2)

Receptionist 2 could be played by the same person who plays Receptionist 1.

(A desk with a sign "MESSAGE IN A GADGET – REGISTER HERE". A young woman, in business attire, is sitting behind a desk. Another young woman, in artistic attire, approaches the desk, holding a rubber duck with various mechanical attachments, they give it the appearance of a rubber duck gadget.)

RECEPTIONIST 2 *(without looking up)*

Can I help you?

YOUNG WOMAN *(speaks very quickly, uses expressive gestures to emphasize what she says)*

Yes, you can, actually. I bought this cute little rubber ducky at a flea market last year in Paris and added a little bit of this and a little bit of that to it and thought about using it in an installation I was working on at the Gladstone Gallery when just by coincidence I sat down on it, and instead of squeaking, it started talking, but not through its beak, it started talking through my mouth – kind of like speaking in tongues – with this really weird voice…

RECEPTIONIST 2 *(looking up)*

In French?

YOUNG WOMAN

Of course not! In English! And the really, really weird thing about it is that it said all sorts of things I would never dare to say.

RECEPTIONIST 2 *(looking down at something on her desk and starting to make notes)*

Two doors to the left we have a therapist. I suggest…

YOUNG WOMAN *(offended)*

Hey! I don't need any of your bungling social welfare therapists. I have enough high-class therapists of my own, world-renowned psychiatrists, Nobel Prize winners, geniuses. So don't try to sell me some cheesy working-class shrink. I am one of the greatest artists of all time, and I demand the very best…

RECEPTIONIST 2 *(looking at the young woman as if she were crazy)*
So what are you doing here?
YOUNG WOMAN *(holding up her rubber duck)*
I want to register this message in a gadget.
RECEPTIONIST 2 *(looking at her desk again and continuing to write)*
Excuse me, but that is not a gadget.
YOUNG WOMAN *(becoming very upset)*
What do you mean? *(pointing at her duck)* This is a gadget, and it…
RECEPTIONIST 2
No, it isn't.
YOUNG WOMAN *(offended)*
What?
RECEPTIONIST 2
A gadget is a small machine or device which does something useful.
YOUNG WOMAN *(upset)*
My rubber ducky has a message…
RECEPTIONIST 2
Your rubber duck is neither a machine nor a device nor does it have a useful message for anyone.
YOUNG WOMAN*(becoming furious)*
How dare you insult my rubber ducky!
(The young woman points the rubber duck at the receptionist.)
RECEPTIONIST 2
Don't aim your rubber duck at me, please, or I'll have to call security.
YOUNG WOMAN
Go ahead and call security, and I'll give you a show you've never seen before!
RECEPTIONIST 2 *(picks up the phone and talks into the receiver)*
Hello, security?

(The young woman squeezes the rubber duck, it squeaks, then she opens her mouth and keeps it open as long as the rubber duck's "voicemail" is being played. The recorded voice should be guttural and fierce - we should have the impression that it is being spewed from the young woman's open mouth.)

RUBBER DUCK *(still being squeezed and aimed at the receptionist)*

Put that phone down right now, you wicked devil, you serpent, you ancient enemy, depraved in mind and corrupt in heart, you unclean spirit, I cast you out, you cursed dragon, and all the tyranny of the infernal spirits. I crush you under my feet and throw you into the bottomless pit. Depart, you devil! Tremble and flee!

(Receptionist 2 runs off stage, the young woman shuts her mouth and turns her rubber duck, so they are now face-to-face.)

YOUNG WOMAN *(to the rubber duck)*

Wow, that was awesome. Let's go make some art.

(The young woman squeezes the rubber duck.)

RUBBER DUCK

Squeak, squeak.

SCENE 5   JUST MY IMAGINATION

"We like the fear of being scared in a contained environment."Dr. Arthur Hunt, Professor of Communications, University of Tennessee.

(A young girl stands in front of the audience.)

YOUNG GIRL

I was just messing around online, looking up all kinds of stuff, typing in simple words like "scary" and "weird", kind of hoping to find some spooky stuff to give me the creeps. I mean, I don't know about you guys, but sometimes I like to get the creeps, I mean I really love it when something sends shivers down my spine, when I feel the hairs on the back of my neck start to prickle and my arms are full of goose bumps. You know there's lots of stuff that really creeps me out, silhouettes that move slowly, spiders crawling on the ceiling, clowns with evil grins, but the stuff that creeps me out the most is stories about girls in really creepy situations where I can imagine exactly what it would be like, and I get so scared, it's like a living nightmare. Anyway, I was cruising the Internet looking for creepy stuff, and I typed in the words "girl in a box" without really knowing what I was looking for. I mean it just sounded so creepy, and I thought, oh, that's cool. And there were over 4½ billion results like always, but the top results were all about the so-called "girl in the box", a girl named Colleen who was kidnapped when she was 20 by this guy named Cameron and his wife Janice, and they basically kept her in a box like a coffin for about seven years. It sounded so incredibly creepy, I mean, they were driving around with their baby, and they picked up Colleen who was hitchhiking, and she got tortured and all that stuff for seven whole years, and then all of a sudden Janice, that was Cameron's wife, got fed up and freed her. And you would think she'd go home right away, but Colleen called Cameron to tell him she was free, because she was kind of hoping he

49

might say something nice and come and pick her up and take her back to his place. I mean, it wasn't even Colleen who called the cops and reported Cameron. It was Janice. I mean, how awesome is that? And then I started thinking, how it would feel if I got kidnapped and thrown into a box for like seven years. So I imagined this guy with a gun – actually it's just a toy gun – and this girl with a knife – like a plastic knife, but the gun and the knife look real, and they come and put a sack over my head…

(A boy with a toy gun and a girl with a toy knife come up from behind the young girl and put a sack over her head and wind a rope around her arms, tying it loosely, so it doesn't fall off.)

GIRL WITH A KNIFE *(poking the knife against the young girl's belly)*

Don't move until I tell you to move. Understand?

BOY WITH A GUN *(going backstage)*

I'll get the box.

(The young girl with the sack over her head starts squirming.)

GIRL WITH A KNIFE

You hear me? I said don't move, or I'll slit your throat and feed you to the dogs!

(We hear dogs barking in the distance. The young girl with the sack over her head starts squealing.)

GIRL WITH A KNIFE *(holds the knife to the young girl's throat)*

Shut up! You hear me? I swear, I'm gonna cut you up into little pieces and feed you to the pigs! *(to the boy with the gun)* Hey, where's the box, damn it? I'm not gonna wait all day!

BOY WITH A GUN *(bringing the box)*

Sorry. It's really heavy.

GIRL WITH A KNIFE

Open it and put her inside.

BOY WITH A GUN

I didn't think we was gonna put her in it. It's just to scare her, ain't it?

GIRL WITH A KNIFE

You idiot! What else we gonna use it for? Garbage?

BOY WITH A GUN

Garbage? What d'you mean?

GIRL WITH A KNIFE

Just shut up and do what I say!

(The boy with the gun opens the box and puts the young girl inside.)

BOY WITH A GUN *(to the young girl)*

Sorry. I don't wanna hurt you.

GIRL WITH A KNIFE

Shut up and shut the damn box!

(The boy with the gun shuts the box. He and the girl with the knife stand guard on both sides for about ten seconds.)

BOY WITH A GUN

We've had her in that box for seven years now. Ain't that long enough?

GIRL WITH A KNIFE

What are you talking about? We agreed to keep her in there for the rest of her life!

BOY WITH A GUN

But that ain't fair.

GIRL WITH A KNIFE

Fair? You think life's been fair to me?

BOY WITH A GUN *(reaching down and unlocking the box)*

I'm gonna let her out.

GIRL WITH A KNIFE

No, you ain't! You ain't ever gonna let her out.

(She stabs him from a distance – she raises the knife, brings it down, and he – about 1½ meters away – jerks and bends, as if he has been stabbed.)

GIRL WITH A KNIFE

You hear me? You ain't ever gonna let her out!

BOY WITH A GUN *(doubling over, raising his gun)*

What'd you do that for?

GIRL WITH A KNIFE

You're dead, man, you're dead!

BOY WITH A GUN *(pointing his gun at the girl with the knife)*

Bang, bang, you're dead, too.

(The girl with the knife and the boy with the gun fall to the ground. Five seconds of silence, then the box is opened from the inside, and the young girl steps out. She removes the sack from her head.)

YOUNG GIRL

I imagined that I came out of the box after seven years, and my two kidnappers were dead. And then I imagined that dozens of reporters wanted to know what it was like living in a box for seven years, I really didn't know what to say, so I just quoted Colleen: "You... remove yourself from the real situation... and go somewhere else. You go somewhere pleasant, around people you love. Whatever makes you happy." *(beat)* Okay, it didn't really happen to me, (beat) I mean, I imagined the whole thing, but it was somehow cool. And really creepy. Know what I mean?

SCENE 6   MESSAGE IN A GADGET (Part 3)

Receptionist 3 could be played by the same person who plays Receptionist 1/2.

(A desk with a sign "MESSAGE IN A GADGET – REGISTER HERE". A young woman, in business attire, is holding a small package. She takes it to a desk and sits down. She looks at the package for a moment before she opens it.)

RECEPTIONIST 3 *(removing something small from the package)*

I sure hope it works.

(She opens the little package that was inside and pulls out wireless earbuds. She also takes out a tiny brochure with instructions and begins reading them aloud.)

RECEPTIONIST 3 *(reading)*

"Use of WHIZKID EARBUDS will impair your ability to think. Caution is highly recommended when you use WHIZKID EARBUDS while engaging in any intellectual activity that requires your full attention. This product is not a toy. If the product begins to perform or respond independently, discontinue use immediately. Before pairing the WHIZKID EARBUDS with your brain, collect your thoughts and get your head together. Insert first the left and then the right WHIZKID EARBUD in the corresponding ear and distinctly say yes three times in three different languages. When you hear a very loud whistle, press the MFB button on the left or right WHIZKID EARBUD to activate data capture, and 90% of your entire mental capacity will be copied together with 85% of your intellectual potential and stored in the purple WHIZKID EARBUD cloud."

(Receptionist 3 inserts the left and right WHIZKID EARBUDS into her ears and presses the corresponding MFB buttons.)

RECEPTIONIST 3

Yes, jawohl, oui.

(We hear a loud, high-pitched whistle, Receptionist 3 hops slightly on her chair, she then grabs her ears and shuts her eyes. We hear a buzzing sound, her body stiffens and shakes a bit. She opens her eyes again, takes

a deep breath and opens her mouth to say something, but nothing comes out. She removes the earbud in her right ear and presses the MFB button.)

RIGHT EARBUD *(a woman's voice, pleasant, confident, reliable – much like a GPS-voice)*

Data transfer successful. 90% of your mental capacity and 85% of your intellectual potential have been stored in the purple WHIZKID EARBUD cloud. None of the data was copied to the cloud. It is impossible to retrieve the data. I repeat, all data is now in the cloud. It is impossible to retrieve the data or transfer it back to the original source.

RECEPTIONIST 3 *(shocked, frantic)*

What? Transferred? Copied? Retrieve? What does that mean? I don't know. I don't know. I can't think. What was I thinking?

(Receptionist 3 raises the earbud in her hand and examines it. She presses the MFB button.)

RIGHT EARBUD

You were thinking that by conserving your thoughts as well as your ability to think in the purple WHIZKID EARBUD cloud, they would become immortal, a wealth of normally inaccessible biographical knowledge available to the rest of the world until the end of time. End of message *(we hear a loud beep).*

RECEPTIONIST 3 *(puzzled)*

Oh.

(Receptionist 3 removes the left earbud, presses the MFB button and holds it in front of her face.)

LEFT EARBUD *(a man's voice, pleasant, confident, reliable – much like a GPS-voice)*

We will do 90% of your thinking from now on. So sit back and press the MFB button whenever your mind is blank. We have an answer to every question, a response to every comment, a memory for every quiet moment. No more agony when you search for words or names on the tip of your tongue. No more embarrassing pauses when you lose the thread. No more memory loss. We are in control of your mind, at least 85 to 90% of it, so don't worry. Keep cool. And press the MFB button whenever you need to think. End of message *(we hear a loud beep)*.

RECPTIONIST 3 *(stares at the audience, silence, then without expression)*

End of message *(we hear a loud beep)*.

SCENE 7   THE BOOGEYMAN WILL GET YOU...

The Boogeyman (also Bogeyman) – according to the American Heritage Dictionary of the English Language (2016) – is "an imaginary evil character of supernatural powers, esp. a mythical hobgoblin, supposed to carry off naughty children." Almost every culture has its own boogeyman to keep kids in line: Roogaroo (French), El Coco (Spanish), L'huomo Nero (Italian), Ou-wu (Chinese), Gryla (Icelandic), Baba Yaga (Russian), Qalupalik (Inuit).

(We hear nighttime sounds: owls hooting, wolves howling, leaves rustling, etc. A person – the boogeyman – appears on stage – male or female – with a small suitcase and a portable luggage rack. The person sets up the luggage rack in front of the audience and places the small suitcase on the luggage rack.)

BOOGEYMAN *(speaking directly to the audience)*

Hi, I'm the boogeyman. *(waves, smiles)* Most of you know me, but you've probably never seen me. At least, not like this.

(The boogeyman opens the suitcase and pulls out a black hooded robe.)

In fact, I'm imaginary, so if you think you have seen me, you certainly just imagined me.

(The boogeyman puts on the black hooded robe.)

Some people think I look like a wolf and eat children.

(The bogeyman starts putting on makeup to quickly create a scary face – a mask could also do the trick.)

Others think of me as a ghost with a pumpkin head or a witch who kidnaps children when they misbehave or a creature with long nails, sharp teeth and long hair that takes children away to live with them under the sea.

(The transformation should have taken place by now. The boogeyman now looks like a boogeyman.)

In any case, I'm the one your parents call when they are at their wit's end. I'm the babysitter no child will ever forget.

(The boogeyman laughs a loud and creepy laugh – which could be substituted by the recording of a loud and creepy laugh.)

BOOGEYMAN

Ha, ha, ha!

(The lights flicker and dim, the boogeyman whips his/her cape around and disappears behind a curtain. Girls 1-3 and Boys 1-3 appear where the boogeyman disappeared. Three of them, Boy 1, Girl 1 and Boy 2, move in single file to positions alongside the audience stage right. The other three, Girl 2, Boy 3 and Girl 3, move in single file to positions alongside the audience stage left. The moment they appear, we hear Brahms' lullaby, either sung by the six performers or as a recording. A music box with the melody might also be a nice addition and a fitting prop for the boogeyman.)

BRAHMS' LULLABY

Lullaby, and good night
With pink roses bedight
With lilies o'er spread
Is my baby's sweet head
Lay you down now, and rest
May your slumber be blessed
Lay you down now, and rest
May your slumber be blessed!

(Girls 1-3 and Boys 1-3 should hold a pose and freeze when the music ends.)

GIRL 1 *(uses the same gestures and movements every time she tells her story)*

When I go to bed, I take a running leap and jump onto my mattress, because he might grab my ankles. Because he's under my bed. That's why I never get up and go to the bathroom at night, because he's always there. The boogeymann.

BOY 1 *(uses the same gestures and movements every time he tells his story)*

My mother puts me to bed, she tells me to stay there, or my dad will spank me. But I get up again, 'cause I'm scared, and I go to the living-room where my parents are watching TV. My father gives me a few swats on the butt and yells at me, and my mom tells me to get back to bed real fast, 'cause the boogeyman is coming, and he'll take me away if I'm not asleep. But I can't fall asleep, 'cause I think I hear him coming, you know, the boogeyman. I hear him breathing.

GIRL 2 *(uses the same gestures and movements every time she tells her story)*

I always fall asleep with the light on, because I know the moment I turn it off he will be there, the boogeyman will jump on me and put a pillow over my head, so I can't breathe, and I will be dead when my mom comes in the next morning to wake me.

BOY 2 *(uses the same gestures and movements every time he tells his story)*

I am scared at night. I feel like something bad might happen. It is so dark in my room. The shadows look like people. Sometimes I hear things in the house and I think the boogeyman is coming.

GIRL 3 *(uses the same gestures and movements every time she tells her story)*

I think I see things in the shadows. I hear noises that scare me. I wonder when my parents are going to go to bed. I wonder when they are going to leave me. I worry that the boogeyman might try to kidnap me. I have a hard time breathing.

BOY 3 *(uses the same gestures and movements every time he tells his story)*

I feel my heart pounding. I worry I might be sick. I worry I might die if I go to sleep. I worry something bad will happen to my parents when I go to sleep. I worry they might leave the house when I am sleeping, and I will be all alone. Maybe he's watching me. Maybe he's in my closet. Maybe he's outside my window, waiting.

(The boogeyman starts creeping around behind the 3 boys and 3 girls, he/she turns swiftly now and then, letting his/her cape sweep around in a full circle.)

GIRL 3

I don't like my closet. I don't like my bed by the window.

BOY 3

I am not tired. I don't like sleeping. I don't want to go to bed.

BOY 1

I have to fall asleep before he comes, but I can't fall asleep.

GIRL 2

Oh, dear God, help me fall asleep. Jesus, Mother Mary, help me fall asleep. Help me.

BOY 2

What's that? I saw something. I think I saw something.

GIRL 1

I hear him breathing under my bed. Listen... *(beat)* Did you hear that? He called my name.

BOOGEYMAN *(laughs his/her creepy laugh, the lullaby ends)* Ha! Ha! Ha!

(The boogeyman continues creeping around behind the 3 boys and 3 girls, turning swiftly now and then, letting his cape sweep around in a full circle, and as he/she passes behind each boy or girl, they line up behind him and follow him/her, desperately and repeatedly whispering their text. Simultaneously, with the same gestures as before.)

BOY 1

My mother puts me to bed, she tells me to stay there, or my dad will spank me. But I get up again, 'cause I'm scared, and I go to the living-room where my parents are watching TV. My father gives me a few swats on the butt and yells at me, and my mom tells me to get back to bed real fast, 'cause the boogeyman is coming, and he'll take me away if I'm not asleep. But I can't fall asleep, 'cause I think I hear him coming, you know, the boogeyman. I hear him breathing.

GIRL 1

When I go to bed, I take a running leap and jump onto my mattress, because he might grab my ankles. Because he's under my bed. That's why I never get up and go to the bathroom at night, because he's always there. The boogeyman.

BOY 2

I am scared at night. I feel like something bad might happen. It is so dark in my room. The shadows look like people. Sometimes I hear things in the house and I think the boogeyman is coming.

GIRL 2

I always fall asleep with the light on, because I know the moment I turn it off he will be there, the boogeyman will jump on me and put a pillow over my head, so I can't breathe, and I will be dead when my mom comes in the next morning to wake me.

BOY 3

I feel my heart pounding. I worry I might be sick. I worry I might die if I go to sleep. I worry something bad will happen to my parents when I go to sleep. I worry they might leave the house when I am sleeping, and I will be all alone. Maybe he's watching me. Maybe he's in my closet. Maybe he's outside my window, waiting.

GIRL 3

I think I see things in the shadows. I hear noises that scare me. I wonder when my parents are going to go to bed. I wonder when they are going to leave me. I worry that the bogeyman might try to kidnap me. I have a hard time breathing.

(The boogeyman returns to his/her props in front of the audience where he/she remains standing, Girls 1-3 and Boys 1-3 move past him/her, still whispering their texts. Girls 1-3 and Boys 1-3 circle the audience on their own, while the boogeyman begins to pack his/her props. Girls 1-3 and Boys 1-3 become louder, as they recite their texts. By the time they have circled the audience, they are nearly shouting. The boogeyman claps his/her hands, and the boys and girls hush at once. They stand side-by-side in front of the

boogeyman with their backs to the audience. They bow their heads as the boogeyman recites his/her lyrics.)

BOOGEYMAN *(in a sing-song, instrumental version of Brahm's Lullaby as background music)*

Lullaby, all my dears

In your eyes I see fear

May your screams cause unrest,

May your dreams be obsessed

Lullaby and good night,

You are boogeyman's delight

No one shields you from harm,

When you sleep in my arms

(The boogeyman laughs his/her creepy laugh, sweeps his/her cape over the heads of the boys and girls, and they disappear backstage.)

BOOGEYMAN (to the audience)

Ha, ha, ha. Good night, sleep tight, and remember: The boogeyman will get you… if you don't watch out.

(The boogeyman laughs his/her creepy laugh.)

BOOGEYMAN

Ha, ha, ha!

(Then he disappears backstage with all his/her props.)

SCENE 8 DON'T TOUCH ME

"Transgenerational trauma, or intergenerational trauma, is a psychological term which asserts that trauma can be transferred in between generations. After a first generation of survivors experiences trauma, they are able to transfer their trauma to their children and further generations of offspring via complex post-traumatic stress disorder mechanisms." – Wikipedia, Oct. 2020

(Mary Jane, a young woman in nondescript clothing, walks across the stage, pushing a baby carriage. She stops, thinks for a moment, lets go of the baby carriage, then she walks back again without the baby carriage. When she gets to the other side, she stops, thinks for a moment, then she walks across the stage again, looks inside the baby carriage, then she grabs it abruptly and pushes it back across the stage. Passerby 1, a young woman in old-fashioned clothes from the 1940s or 1950s, approaches from the other side. They walk past each other. Mary Jane keeps on walking, Passerby 1 stops, thinks for a moment, turns around…)

PASSERBY 1 *(calling out to Mary Jane)*

Mary Ellen?… Mary Ellen! Is that you?

(Mary Jane stops.)

PASSERBY 1

Mary Ellen? Remember me?

MARY JANE *(looks confused, annoyed)*

Excuse me?

PASSERBY 1 *(walks towards Mary Jane, stops in front of her)*

I'm Helen. Helen Reed. We went to school together. We were best friends until you moved away.

(Passerby 1 reaches out to touch Mary Jane on the shoulder.)

PASSERBY 1 *(touching Mary Jane on the shoulder)*

We did everything together…

MARY JANE *(interrupting Passerby 1, jerking away)*

Don't touch me.

PASSERBY 1

Sorry, I didn't mean to…

MARY JANE

And my name is not Mary Ellen. It's Mary Jane.

PASSERBY 1

I'm really very sorry. It's just that you remind me of my dear friend Mary Ellen.

MARY JANE

My grandmother's name was Mary Ellen.

PASSERBY 1

Your grandmother? Oh. What a coincidence.

MARY JANE

Coincidence? What do you mean?

PASSERBY 1

That my best friend and your grandmother have the same name.

MARY JANE

So what?

PASSERBY 1

And you look just like Mary Ellen.

MARY JANE

What are you trying to say?

PASSERBY 1

That it's a coincidence.

MARY JANE

My grandmother died 10 years ago. When I was 9. She was an angry woman, a mean woman, a woman who hated life.

PASSERBY 1

The Mary Ellen I knew was kind and generous. She was a wonderful girl, a beautiful girl who loved life.

MARY JANE

I hated her for the way she treated my mother. For the way she neglected my mother. For the way she emotionally deserted my mother.

PASSERBY 1

Mary Ellen moved away after her father died and her mother remarried.

MARY JANE

I hated my grandmother with all my heart until I found her diary.

PASSERBY 1

The last time she wrote she said that something terrible had happened, but she couldn't talk about it.

MARY JANE

She wrote that a man abused her. Again and again. He beat her, and he sexually abused her, and he let other men abuse her, and her mother knew about it, but she didn't say anything. She told her mother, but she didn't do anything. She let it happen.

PASSERBY 1

I always felt it had something to do with her stepfather.

MARY JANE

And when she was 16 she became pregnant.

PASSERBY 1

Someone told me they had seen her with a baby.

MARY JANE

It was my mother. The child she had was my mother. She named her Mary Beth.

PASSERBY 1

So Mary Beth is your mother?

MARY JANE

Yes.

PASSERBY 1

And Mary Ellen was your grandmother?

MARY JANE

Yes. And I am Mary Jane.

PASSERBY 1 *(looking inside the baby carriage for the first time)*

And whose baby is that?

(Mary Jane doesn't answer. She looks away.)

PASSEBY 1

Well, I'm sorry for this misunderstanding, Mary Jane. Have a nice day.

(Passerby 1 walks away. Mary Jane shakes her head and pushes the baby carriage to the other side of the stage. She stops, thinks for a moment, looks inside the baby carriage, then she walks back across the stage again with the baby carriage. When she gets to the other

side, she stops, thinks for a moment, lets go of the baby carriage, then she walks across the stage again without the baby carriage. Passerby 2, a young woman in psychedelic clothes from the early 1970s, approaches from the other side. They walk past each other. Mary Jane keeps on walking, Passerby 2 stops, thinks for a moment, turns around…)

PASSERBY 2 *(calling out to Mary Jane)*

Mary Beth?… Mary Beth! Is that you?

(Mary Jane stops.)

PASSERBY 2

Mary Beth? Remember me?

MARY JANE *(looks confused, annoyed)*

Excuse me?

PASSERBY 2 *(walks towards Mary Jane, stops in front of her)*

I'm Martha. Martha Sloan. We went to college together. We were best friends until you got pregnant.

(Passerby 2 reaches out to touch Mary Jane on the shoulder.)

PASSERBY 2 *(touching Mary Jane on the shoulder)*

We had so much fun together…

MARY JANE *(interrupting Passerby 2, jerking away)*

Don't touch me.

PASSERBY 2

Sorry, I didn't mean to…

MARY JANE

And my name is not Mary Beth. It's Mary Jane.

PASSERBY 2

I'm really very sorry. It's just that you remind me of my dear friend Mary Beth.

MARY JANE

My mother's name was Mary Beth.

PASSERBY 2

Your mother? Oh. What a coincidence.

MARY JANE

Coincidence? What do you mean?

PASSERBY 2

That my best friend and your mother have the same name.

MARY JANE

So what?

PASSERBY 2

And you look just like Mary Beth.

MARY JANE

What are you trying to say?

PASSERBY 2

That it's a coincidence.

MARY JANE

My mother is dead.

PASSERBY 2

I'm sorry to hear that. The Mary Beth I knew was pregnant and had a baby, and I never saw her again.

MARY JANE

She killed herself.

PASSERBY 2

Your mother?

MARY JANE

She wanted to be a good mother, but she was always so tired, so unhappy, so… so… miles away.

PASSERBY 2

The Mary Beth I knew was kind of shy at first. Naïve and afraid of something. But then we moved into a commune together with my boyfriend, and she started opening up and having fun.

MARY JANE

My mother never laughed. When I was good, she called me her angel, but when I was bad, she locked herself in her room for hours. She never let me play outside, because she was afraid something terrible might happen to me.

PASSERBY 2

That's when she got pregnant. But she didn't know who the father was. You know, free love and stuff. Maybe it was my boyfriend, I don't know. And that's when she freaked out and went back to live with her mother.

MARY JANE

I never had a father. My mother never talked about him.

PASSERBY 2

Just you and your mother and your grandmother?

MARY JANE

My grandmother killed herself when I was 9.

PASSERBY 2

And when did your mother kill herself?

MARY JANE

Last year. When I got pregnant.

PASSERBY 2 *(looks across the stage at the baby carriage)*

Is that your baby?

(Mary Jane looks away and doesn't reply.)

PASSERBY 2

Okay. Sorry about the misunderstanding.

(Passerby 2 gazes at Mary Jane for a long moment, then she walks away. The moment she is gone, Mary Jane walks over to the baby carriage and pushes it back across the stage. While she is doing so, Passerby 3, a young female in nondescript clothes, appears on the opposite side of the stage – where the baby carriage had been standing – and watches Mary Jane.)

PASSERBY 3 *(watching Mary Jane and calling to her)*

Mary Jane?… Mary Jane! Is that you?

(Mary Jane stops and turns around.)

PASSERBY 3

Mary Jane? Remember me?

MARY JANE *(looks confused, annoyed, seems to hide the baby carriage behind her back)*

Excuse me?

PASSERBY 3 *(walks towards Mary Jane, stops in front of her)*

I'm Janet. Janet Rusley. We went to school together. I was in some of your classes.

(Passerby 3 reaches out to touch Mary Jane on the shoulder.)

PASSERBY 3 *(touching Mary Jane on the shoulder)*

We never really did anything together…

MARY JANE *(interrupting Passerby 1, jerking away)*
Don't touch me.
PASSERBY 3
Sorry, I didn't mean to…
MARY JANE
You remember me?
PASSERBY 3
Yeah. I always liked you.
MARY JANE
You liked me?
PASSERBY 3
'cause you were different. So quiet. Kind of mysterious. But it was impossible to get close to you.
MARY JANE
I'm really very sorry… Janet.
PASSERBY 1
Janet Rusley. I even sat next to you in Spanish. You were a very good student.
MARY JANE
I wanted to please my mother. I wanted her to be proud. I wanted her to like me.
PASSERBY 3
How did it happen?
MARY JANE
She overdosed.
PASSERBY 3
No, I mean…
(Passerby 3 nods at the baby carriage.)
MARY JANE
What do you mean?
PASSERBY 3
You were such a good student, and then you suddenly dropped out of school, and somebody said they saw you with bandages around your wrists, and now this…
(Passerby 3 nods at the baby carriage again.)

MARY JANE

What do you want from me?

PASSERBY 3

I told you, I like you, Mary Jane. I'd like to help you.

(Passerby 3 reaches out to touch Mary Jane on the shoulder.)

MARY JANE *(jerking away)*

I told you not to touch me!

PASSERBY 3

I'm sorry, I just wanted to…

MARY JANE

Just mind your own business, and leave me alone!

(Mary Jane stomps off stage, Passerby 3 watches her walk away. She feels helpless. After Mary Jane is gone, she turns around and realizes that Mary Jane has left the baby carriage behind. She panics.)

PASSERBY 3 *(yelling)*

Mary Jane! Wait! Your baby! You forgot your baby!

(Passerby 3 looks around, she has no clue.)

PASSERBY 3

What do I do?

(Once again she looks around, then she cautiously looks inside the baby carriage. She reaches into the baby carriage and pulls the "baby" out. She holds it up.)

PASSERBY 3 *(holding up a doll)*

No way! This is incredible! Absurd! A doll! She's pushing a doll around in a baby carriage! That's sick! It's insane!

(Passerby 3 throws the doll into the baby carriage.)

PASSERBY 3

I always thought she was weird!

(She stomps off stage. Almost simultaneously Mary Jane appears from the other side of the stage. She walks over to the baby carriage and looks in.)

MARY JANE *(reaching into the baby carriage and pulling out the doll)*

Hey little one, it's time for dinner.

(Mary Jane holds up the doll and gazes affectionately at her.)

You know something, Mary Margaret. I love you more than anything or anyone in the whole world.

(Mary Jane puts the doll in the baby carriage and pushes it offstage.)

SCENE 9   A FATE WORSE THAN FEAR

(A classroom, semi-darkness. Shadows and shafts of light irregularly crisscross the room, occasional flashes of red and blue light. We hear muffled sounds from outside: sirens, shouting, gunshots, screams – a surrealistic overture, a stifled chamber-of-horrors scenario. Scattered silhouettes of tables and chairs become visible, some standing, some overturned – a room in disarray. Here and there we detect undefinable shapes on the floor: some clumped, some flat – blobs of darkness. We hear a typing sound, then we see a text message projected onto a screen - either behind the actors, to the side of the stage or as a transparent projection screen. Other text messages follow.)

TEXT MESSAGE 1 *(projected onto screen)*

I don't know if it's a drill or not.

TEXT MESSAGE 2 *(projected onto screen)*

I'm so scared. I love you, Mommy.

TEXT MESSAGE 3 *(projected onto screen)*

We're in lockdown. I hear sirens and police cars.

TEXT MESSAGE 4 *(projected onto screen)*

I'm having a panic attack.

TEXT MESSAGE 5 *(projected onto screen)*

Something's happened, shooters maybe.

TEXT MESSAGE 6 *(projected onto screen)*

I'm in a classroom.

TEXT MESSAGE 7 *(projected onto screen)*

Keep texting me, please.

(We hear a ringtone, then another one overlaps, then another one, then another one, then another one, then another one, then another one – each one is quickly turned off. Silence. The text messages disappear. Gradually one of the blobs begins to move.)

RACHEL *(lying on the floor, sits up)*

I'm Rachel.

CASSIE *(hunched behind a chair)*

Hey, Rachel, it's me, Cassie.

RACHEL

Hi, Cassie. Who else is here?

DAN *(sits up)*

I'm Dan. I'm in 10th grade.

KELLEY *(sits up)*

I'm in 10th grade, too. I think I know you.

DAN *(turns to Kelley)*

What's your name?

KELLEY *(turns to Dan)*

Kelley.

DAN

Oh yeah. Hi, Kelley.

JOHN *(sits up)*

My name's John. We just moved here, and today's my first day at school.

LAUREN *(turns to John)*

What a lousy first day. Sorry about that, John. My name's Lauren, by the way.

ISAIAH *(sits up)*

And I'm Isaiah.

KELLEY *(turns to Isaiah)*

Isaiah Stone? The football player?

ISAIAH *(turns to Kelley)*

Yeah.

KELLEY

That's cool. My kid brother thinks you're the greatest. Can I have your autograph?

ISAIAH

Sure, if we ever get out of here alive.

LAUREN

Oh God!

RACHEL *(looks around)*

Does anybody know what's going on?

(Loud pounding. Everyone lies on the floor. It sounds as if someone is beating against the classroom door. Screaming. Gunshots. One piercing gunshot, Isaiah jerks and bumps against a chair. Footsteps walking away. Silence.)

TEXT MESSAGE 8 *(projected onto screen)*

They just shot through the walls.

TEXT MESSAGE 9 *(projected onto screen)*

I'm really scared.

TEXT MESSAGE 10 *(projected onto screen)*

Don't call, please.

TEXT MESSAGE 11 *(projected onto screen)*

No idea what's going on.

TEXT MESSAGE 12 *(projected onto screen)*

I love you so much.

TEXT MESSAGE 13 *(projected onto screen)*

I'm safe now, I think.

TEXT MESSAGE 14 *(projected onto screen)*

I just got hit by a bullet.

(Silence. The text messages disappear.)

KELLEY *(whispering)*

I think they're gone.

ISAIAH *(groaning)*

Oh God, it hurts.

KELLEY

Isaiah, is that you?

ISAIAH

Yeah.

KELLEY

What happened?

ISAIAH

I think I got shot in the arm.

LAUREN

Are you bleeding?

ISAIAH

Yeah.

DAN

Lots of blood?

ISAIAH

No. I think the bullet just grazed me.

JOHN

I'm really good at first aid. Want me to have a look?

ISAIAH

No. Better stay where you are. You never know.

KELLEY

Does it hurt?

ISAIAH

Yeah, I feel a bit dizzy. I'll just put my feet up.

(Isaiah lies down on his back and puts his feet on a chair.)

RACHEL

Does anybody know what's going on?

(We hear loud explosions, more sirens, screaming. Silence.)

TEXT MESSAGE 15 *(projected onto screen)*

What's going on?

TEXT MESSAGE 16 *(projected onto screen)*

I can't stop shaking.

TEXT MESSAGE 17 *(projected onto screen)*

If I don't get outta here alive, tell Dad how much I love you guys.

TEXT MESSAGE 18 *(projected onto screen)*

Help me, please. I'm having a panic attack.

TEXT MESSAGE 19 *(projected onto screen)*

I feel sick to my stomach.

TEXT MESSAGE 20 *(projected onto screen)*

No more ammo, still have the explosives.

TEXT MESSAGE 21 *(projected onto screen)*

Where are the police?

(Silence. The text messages disappear.)

LAUREN

Is this for real?

JOHN

A real school shooting?

DAN

First time for me.

LAUREN

For me, too.

JOHN

Third.

LAUREN

What?

JOHN

My third time.

LAUREN

You gotta be kidding.

JOHN

Seems like every school I go to there's a school shooting.

LAUREN

Sounds like bad karma.

JOHN

Good luck.

RACHEL

Were many people killed?

JOHN

The first time just three. A teacher, a janitor and one of my classmates.

RACHEL

That must have been terrible. Did you know all three of them?

JOHN

Yeah.

KELLEY

What a coincidence. Three school shootings. That must be a world record or something.

JOHN

Destiny.

CASSIE

Destiny?

DAN

And the second one?

JOHN

What?

DAN

The second school shooting? How many people were killed?

JOHN

Five.

RACHEL

Did you know them?

JOHN

Sure. They were all sitting at my table in the cafeteria.

LAUREN

You gotta be kidding.

DAN

At lunch?

JOHN

Yeah.

RACHEL

Wait a minute. I read about that. The killer texted everybody to meet him at that table. They were his friends. He was angry at some girl, because she refused to date him.

JOHN

She asked for it.

(Silence.)

CASSIE

Oh yeah?

RACHEL

She was killed, too.

JOHN *(to Rachel)*

How do you know so much about it, Rachel?

RACHEL

I read a lot. I try to understand how people can be so mean. I want to help…

JOHN

A do-gooder?

RACHEL

I try to do what's right.

JOHN

A believer?

RACHEL

I believe in God, if that's what…

JOHN

Then you'd better start praying.

CASSIE

What did you say?

JOHN

Pray, Rachel. That's what Christians do, don't they? Pray, baby, pray! Pray, baby, pray!

RACHEL

Stop it, John!

ISAIAH *(groaning slightly, obviously in pain)*

Hey, what's your problem, John?

JOHN

Is that Mr. Tough Guy, Isaiah? How's your arm? Bleeding to death over there?

DAN

Shut up, John, or I'll come over and shut you up!

JOHN

I wouldn't try it, big boy.

DAN

Oh yeah? Why not?

JOHN

I have some pretty powerful Semtex attached to my belt…

DAN

What are you talking about?

JOHN

Explosives. Enough to blow us all to smithereens.

KELLEY

Oh my God! Are you…?

JOHN

One of them?

KELLEY

… a school shooter?

JOHN

What do you think?

LAUREN

What are you doing here?

JOHN

Hiding like the rest of you.

ISAIAH

Hiding from yourself?

JOHN

Good joke.

KELLEY

Oh my God! I don't believe it!

RACHEL

Why are you doing this?

JOHN

Why do we do anything, Rachel?

RACHEL

What do you mean?

JOHN

Destiny.

RACHEL

God's will.

JOHN

I prefer to call it destiny. I'm the chosen one.

CASSIE

Chosen to do what?

JOHN

To take you all with me.

LAUREN

You're out of your mind.

JOHN

No, you're outta your minds to put up with your fake lives in your fake families, going to your fake schools every day!

(Silence.)

ISAIAH

What if we don't want to go with you?

JOHN

What?

ISAIAH

What if we don't want to go with you when you blow yourself to smithereens?

JOHN

You don't have a choice now, do you?

(We hear electronic beeps.)

RACHEL

What are you doing?

JOHN

Setting the timer.

KELLEY

Oh my God! I don't believe it!

RACHEL

Stop this nonsense right now, John.

DAN

What right do you have coming in here and…

JOHN *(getting upset)*

No rights! No rights at all! From the moment I was born and even before that, it was determined, it was decided, and I was chosen to do it!

CASSIE

Do what?

JOHN

If it moves, kill it.

LAUREN

What are you talking about?

JOHN

Don't follow your dreams or gods or any of that shit, follow your animal instincts.

DAN

You're full of shit, John!

JOHN

Our schools and our laws beat it out of us. They destroy our instincts. Society makes us all the same parasitical wimps. You know, if you stick to your instincts, they call you a psycho or a lunatic.

CASSIE

You're crazy, John!

JOHN

You parasites and retards are never gonna understand my motives. You're gonna say, "He's crazy, he's insane, he's worthless!" But like Nietzsche said, "The weak and the failures shall perish!" You guys are gonna die! And I'm gonna take you with me.

RACHEL

Dear God, hear us in this hour of darkness…

JOHN

God is dead, Jesus is dead … get over it! Thank God they crucified him!

RACHEL

Stop it!

DAN

You are the most disgusting person…

JOHN

Evil.

DAN

What?

JOHN

I am the most evil person you have ever met. And I am in power! Because I am armed! I am strong!

ISAIAH

Weak!

JOHN

Strong and powerful. Like God. It is you who are weak. And I disdain weakness. I want to just tear some little high school kid apart and show them who is God. Ever hear of Charles Manson?

LAUREN

You are sick.

JOHN

I am evil. And I will inherit the earth, because the strongest and most evil spirits shall rule the world!

KELLEY

Tell me this isn't true! Tell me it's just a nightmare! Tell me I'm gonna wake up and...

CASSIE

Calm down, Kelley.

JOHN

Ten.

RACHEL *(reciting the Apostles' Creed)*

I believe in God, the Father Almighty...

JOHN *(overlapping, loud)*

Nine.

RACHEL *(we only hear fragments of the Creed)*

... maker of heaven and earth, and in Jesus Christ, our Lord...

JOHN *(overlapping, loud)*

Eight.

RACHEL

... conceived by the Holy Spirit, born of the Virgin Mary...

CASSIE

This is just a joke, isn't it?

JOHN *(overlapping, loud)*

Seven.

RACHEL

... crucified, died and was buried...

JOHN *(overlapping, loud)*

Six.

RACHEL

... ascended into heaven...

JOHN *(overlapping, loud)*

Five.

RACHEL

... to judge the living...

KELLEY

We're going to die!

JOHN *(overlapping, loud)*

Four.

RACHEL

… I believe in the holy spirit…

CASSIE

Stop it! Stop it!

JOHN *(overlapping, loud)*

Three.

RACHEL

… the forgiveness of sins…

JOHN *(overlapping, loud)*

Two.

RACHEL

… and the life everlasting…

JOHN *(overlapping, loud)*

One.

RACHEL

Amen.

(Silence.)

JOHN

Bang!

DAN

What?

JOHN *(bursts out laughing)*

Just kidding, guys. You didn't really believe me, did you?

KELLEY

My God, I don't believe it!

ANNOUNCEMENT *(via loudspeaker)*

Attention, attention, all students and staff, this lockdown is now all-clear. I repeat, this lockdown is all-clear. The lockdown has been lifted.

(The lights go on. All the students but John slowly get up. Kelley helps Isaiah get to his feet. John remains seated on the floor. The

door opens, and all the students but John slowly leave the classroom. They all look straight ahead or down at the floor, seemingly shocked and lost in thought. The last to leave is Rachel. She turns...

RACHEL

John...

(John holds up a hand and points his index finger at Rachel.)

RACHEL

If you like, we could...

(John cocks his thumb, as if his hand were a gun.)

JOHN *(aiming his "gun" at Rachel, loud and clear)*

Bang!

(Lights out.)

ABOUT THE AUTHOR

John Reed Middleton was born in Cedar Rapids, Iowa (USA). He was a teacher for 43 years at a German school in Hamburg where he taught English, Drama and Art. He has also spent over 35 years subtitling films and translating screenplays (www.middleton-group-translations.com).

During the past 30 years he has performed his own five one-act plays (DAVID, THE DEATH OF A CLOWN, CARNIVAL AT CASTLE ROCK, KILLING DADDY, LITTLE GOETHE and DAS KLEID) at small theaters in and around Hamburg.

THE PLAYLET SERIES is his latest writing project, topical collections of scenes in English for English learners from Year 1 to Year 12 (Level 1 to Level 6) who want to perform (english-playlets.com).

By purchasing the play, you automatically obtain the stage rights.